The Best of "60 Seconds on Officiating"
is published in the United States
by X60 MEDIA, LLC

© 2013 by X60 MEDIA, LLC

Created by Al Battista, Tim Malloy, and Billy Martin

For Official /Umpire resources, visit:
www.ref60.com
www.refereelife.com

Necessary corrections and subsequent updates
can be found at:
www.gobeyondtherules.com

ISBN: 978-1494306687
First Printing: December 2013

Forward

When we launched "60 Seconds on Officiating" six years ago, our goal was to shatter the basketball rulebook and present the pieces in an easy-to-absorb, "reality-based" manner that would attract referees, and anyone else in the global basketball community, who preferred to take in their knowledge of the rules in small but steady doses.

Every topic posted on our **REF 60** website (www.Ref60.com) presented to make that piece of the game easier to understand, easier to remember, and we believe, easier to rule for an official when the situation presents itself in a game.

In addition to serving up the rules in palatable portions, our "60 Seconds" posts also offer meaningful game managements strategies and styles that have been practiced successfully by some the officiating leaders in the game today.

And our newest publication, *"The Best of 60 Seconds on Officiating"* has bundled the prime cuts of our web and email posts and presents them as another powerful reference tool to help build your officiating career.

We take great pride in making sure every measure of content created under our *"60 Seconds on Officiating"* teaching umbrella, is done so with the critical understanding that officials must be mindful of "sharpening their axe" in order to deliver their best performance in every game they are assigned.

Because the painful reality for all of us is, there is no standing still, or staying the same. You are either getting better or you're getting worse...

The status quo, as it were, and those who find comfort in it, are being downsized and moved out on a daily basis. Like the proverbial under-performing lumberjack who was, *'too busy to take time to sharpen his axe;'* no official can afford to embrace the approach of being too busy working games to take time to sharpen their understanding of the rules and their proper application.

So we invite you to put your nose, as well as your eyes, to our latest literary grindstone – **The Best of 60 Seconds on Officiating** – and watch your sharpened officiating abilities break free of the gravitational pull to mediocrity on your way to obscurity, and push through to a level of superiority that will have you and your polished talents in demand by assignors, favored by coaches and welcomed by spectators.

Yours in officiating,

Al Battista, Tim Malloy, and Billy Martin

About the Authors

Al Battista is first and foremost an educator, and his passion for basketball officiating and his desire to share his in-depth knowledge on the subject has been utilized at all levels of the game.

Al is a 36+ year respected member of IAABO and a dual member of Board 215 (West Virginia) and Board 12 (Washington D.C.), and currently serves with distinction in the high school and college ranks as the Interpreter for the West Virginia Intercollegiate Athletic Conference (WVIAC), the Pennsylvania State Athletic Conference (PSAC), the Capital Athletic Conference (CAC), the Maryland Junior College Conference, and is on the IAABO Rules Examination Committee. In the professional game, Al has been a staff observer for the NBA and WNBA since 2004 and 2007, respectively.

Al also is the creator and editor of the highly-respected officiating newsletter, MATCH UP and was on staff with the MEAC for 26 years while earning three "Sweet 16" round assignments in the NCAA Division III tournament. Al currently is a member of CBOA and the Big South Staff.

About the Authors

Tim Malloy, between the ebb and flow of a chronic illness that has required 32 surgeries, has pushed forward and carved a path of distinction in both the world of basketball and business.

As a 40+ year veteran referee of IAABO Board 34, Tim has worked numerous New Jersey state playoff games and climbed the ladder to the college ranks. Tim officiated as a member of CBOA where he earned Division II and III playoff assignments.

Off the court, Tim was a front office executive for the NBA World Champion Philadelphia 76ers in 1983 and served as the team's Assistant Group Sales Director and Public Relations Director for seven seasons. Tim later worked as a Sales and Promotions representative for Converse Inc., where he was a two-time Salesman-of-the Year award winner. He also holds a U.S. Patent for a golf training device that received a 4-star rating in Golf Magazine and is the co-author of the sports reference books, *Blue Book 60* for fast pitch softball.

Tim is a graduate of St. Joseph's University (PA) and resides in Somerdale, NJ with his wife Pattie, son Matt and daughter Mary Frances.

About the Authors

Billy Martin has 35+ years basketball officiating experience for IAABO Camden NJ Board 34 and most recently with Cumberland / Cape Board 196 in Southern, NJ.

He previously served as Board 34's Supervisor of Officials for the 300- member organization and was responsible for official's ratings and education.

In the business world, Billy has more than 30 years of sales and marketing experience, and currently works with Salesforce.com, the industry leader in Customer Relationship Management and Marketing tools.

Billy holds a Master's Degree in Education (MEd) from The College of New Jersey specializing in Sports Medicine and a Master's Degree in Business Administration (MBA) from the University of Phoenix in Technology Management.

Additionally, Billy is a collegiate fast-pitch softball umpire for the East Coast Softball Umpires Association, along with being a scholastic umpire with West Chapter 5 and the USSSA of Southern NJ. He is the co-author of the widely respected rules education book titled, *Blue Book 60- Fast Pitch Edition* which can be found at www.bluebook60.com.

Billy has three daughters – Jennifer, Jessica, and Alissa while enjoying the sand between his toes living in Wildwood, NJ.

References

Please refer directly to the official rule sets for each organization, as this publication is not intended to replace the official publications of these associations.

(NFHS) -- National Federation of State High School Associations

The NFHS, from its offices in Indianapolis, Indiana, serves its 50- member state high school athletic/activity associations, plus the District of Columbia. The NFHS publishes playing rules in 16 sports for boys and girls reaching 18,500 high schools and over 11 million students involved in athletic and activity programs.

NFHS Publications Order Department – www.nfhs.org
P.O. Box 361246
Indianapolis, IN 46236-5324
Phone: (800) 776–3462

(NCAA) -- The National Collegiate Athletic Association

The National Collegiate Athletic Association (NCAA) is a voluntary organization through which the nation's colleges and universities govern their athletics programs.

NCAA Publications Online – www.ncaapublications.com
P.O. Box 6222
Indianapolis, Indiana 46206-6222
Phone: (317) 917-6222

When a Foul is Not a Foul
by Billy Martin

While watching a NCAA Division I basketball game, I witnessed an interesting series of events that I've had numerous "energized" discussions with my colleagues about foul-calling philosophy.

It has to do with three common rule interpretations...

- Incidental Contact
- Intentional Fouls
- Fouling to Stop the Clock
  (toward the end of a game)

The game went something like this.

The visiting team (B) was ahead by a fourteen points with just around 1:30 left in the game. The home team (A) had just made a field goal to cut the score to a 12-point deficit and set up to employ a full court defensive press. Team B's plan was clear -- inbound the ball and play keep away -- as they preferred to run some time off the clock before being forced to the free throw line.

But Team A had other plans, and what happened is typical of what occurs at all levels of play.

Team B inbounded the ball to a speedy guard that was well ahead of the defender who made "incidental contact" with the dribbler at the **EXACT** time the trail official was "loading up" his whistle to rule a back court foul.

My first impression was the dribbler was hardly touched and it was obvious Team B did not want to be fouled and had designs on running some precious time off the clock. My thought was - "was that a foul in the first 10 minutes of the game?" I doubt it was.

As an official, why put the offensive team (B) at a disadvantage here??

By rule incidental contact is clearly defined by both NCAA and NFHS. Incidental contact is contact with an opponent which is permitted and which does NOT constitute a foul per NFHS rules. NCAA is similar; whereas contact that does not hinder the opponent from participating in normal defensive or offensive movements shall be considered incidental.

But the story gets better. Team B is already in the double bonus and misses both free throws. On the second of two - Team B gains possession of the rebound and the player from Team A **"intentionally"** wraps two arms around the waist of the player to quickly foul again. The center official rules a **"common foul"** vs. an intentional foul. Even the announcer is amazed.

Well you can probably guess the outcome of this story. Team B misses a bunch of free throws in that remaining minute and the home team ties it up with just seconds to go. The contest does go to overtime and the visiting team did eventually win ... but it was a bit harder.

I do wonder the following questions:

What is our reluctance (as officials) to call **intentional fouls (NFHS) or flagrant 1 personal fouls (NCAA)** at the end of a game when the coach is yelling to foul and the defender makes no attempt to play the ball and is trying to stop the clock?

What is our rationale for "anticipating" a defensive team fouling --- and rewarding this practice by quickly calling that foul that many times is simply **incidental contact** - gaining no defensive advantage?

A 2013 NFHS Poll asked our opinion on such topics. One suggestion is to allow the defensive team a choice of shooting free throws or inbounding the ball again, when fouled in the bonus. The other is to change the definition of "intentional foul" to add severity and take the subjectivity of "intent" out of the equation. [At press time, none of these changes were implemented in the rule changes for 2014]

My only take away here is ... if you have a patient whistle during the end of a game, you are more likely to allow incidental contact to occur without "blowing." This might not be in line with the thinking of the basketball purist but it will keep a closer balance between offense / defense in the closing minutes competitive game.

Rule References
NFHS 4-27, 4-19-3, 4-28-4 NCAA 4.29.2c, 4.40

Respect is a Two Way Street
by Al Battista

As I come down the home stretch on my 35th season as a basketball official and step back to assess the state of our great game, I am concerned that the dial on boorish and unsportsmanlike behavior is being steadily turned up and doing tremendous damage to the sport we care deeply about.

I've watched this bully mentality take place as a casual spectator at games of all levels, as well as in my role as a high school, college and professional league observer. And I have also been on the receiving end as an official of the often hostile attitude exhibited by players, coaches and fans...It has to stop!

And until we can affect change at the source, it is up to us as referees -- the official gatekeepers for the game -- to hold the line and enforce the rules of conduct, both fairly and firmly.

As the rewards for winning have trickled down into the youth levels of our games, what were once well-intended motives have now been blurred and win at all costs is becoming a dominating sentiment for AAU teams and travel team leagues across the country.

The coddled middle-school player and the pampered high school player are growing in great numbers, thanks in large part to the grandiose expectations of unrealistic parents and the ulterior motives of coaches.

And it is our job as officials to focus on bringing respect back into every game you work.

**Respect...Give it freely,
and demand it unequivocally.**

We honor the game and respect those who coach and play it fairly, and who watch it from the bleachers with a level of decorum, when we firmly deal with those coaches, players and spectators who bring a thug-like approach to the game and attempt to impose their will on it.

While the bad element may be growing in numbers in our game; they rarely out-number the good people in any specific contest who want their officials to handle their business. It is only when the good people feel they are on their own and they must fend for themselves against the bully player, coach or spectator, that chaos breaks out.

When we understand that Dr. James Naismith may have invented a perfect game; it is played, coached and officiated by imperfect people, so mistakes are going to be made by all parties represented at every game!

Coaches, players and even fans, are entitled to expect a certain level of professionalism from the officials working their game. That is to say, their referees should have a thorough knowledge of the rules; be physically capable of keeping up with the level of play and be in proper position to rule on plays; be at least cordial and somewhat friendly, and not antagonistic or confrontational.

And it is within our rights as officials to expect to not feel threatened over any call made, no matter how bad the call may actually be. Your personal safety should never be in question.

It is important to know that we as officials have the power, real power, so there is no need for you to match the level of bluster and bravado of an obnoxious coach, player or spectator.

We can remove a person from the gym; we can clear the entire gym; we can cancel a game; we can summon the police and often bring the full extent of the law crashing down on anyone who crosses way beyond the line.

That is REAL POWER...Use it wisely.

Now in an ideal setting, the athletic leagues and schools would work on building respect for the game with their coaches, players and spectators; and our officiating organizations from Maine to California, and around the world, would produce officials who are excellent game managers who will stand resolutely against those who do not respect the game or their authority, and both sides would meet in the middle and congratulate each other for a job well done.

But until that day comes, the job falls to you to give respect and earn respect to protect our great game...One game at a time.

Respect ....It's a two-way street.

The Problem with Free Throws
by Billy Martin

After watching in person or on online (courtesy of YouTube and several scholastic websites) all or part of quite a few high school games, it was surprising to notice the alarming number of free throw lane violations that were either missed by the officials working the game, or the crew's apparent decision to simply chose to ignore the infractions.

Now this is **NOT** referring to scenarios where players maybe step into the free throw lane area just a split second before the ball touches the rim (this not a discussion on making nit-picking calls); but rather the cases where a player clearly violates the marked lane space provisions and it is not penalized.

And this seems to be the case in about 90% of the games you'll watch from the stands or on television.

When was the last game you watched, or worked, where there was a free throw violation called?

Is it really possible to go an entire game without **ONE** free throw violation?

Possible ... but more unlikely not.

The reason may be is that good officials by nature strive to stay 'in the background' of each game they work and may see making this ruling as a 'game interrupter.' And officials are customer service oriented, meaning, "if the coach isn't asking for it; we aren't calling it."

Whatever the root cause is for the lack of better enforcement of this infraction, here are a few tips to help clarify your understanding of illegal movement during free throws that will hopefully strengthen your resolve to call the obvious lane violations when they occur in your area.

PRE-GAME DISCUSSION: Make `sure your crew discusses free throw coverage and calling violations in your pre-game conferences. Make it a habit to discuss who covers what players and determine what the crew's philosophy will be on calling free throw violations early in the contest to show the crew's commitment to enforcement, so as not make a free throw violation ruling in the second half that wasn't called in the first.

WHEN DO RESTRICTIONS END? Remember players are restricted until the try touches the ring, backboard, or free throw is over. As an NFHS official are you mistakenly thinking it's OK for players to move into the lane area on the release (like NCAA); or are you just subtly deciding to ignore this infraction? If you're passing on making the call where a player gained a clear advantage by committing an infraction (leaving early and securing possession of the ball on a missed free throw), the question becomes, "what other violations are you willing to ignore?

SNEAKY PLAYERS: On the top of the list of free throw violations NOT whistled are the "spin and scoop" moves from players in the 2nd occupied lane spaces. These are the players (of the shooting team) that will spin and sneak behind the opponent in the 1st space, on the release of the free thrower, to gain an unfair advantage. Is this violation being called when it occurs in the games you are working?

ABLE TO EXPLAIN WHAT YOU CALL: Many officials are of the mind set, *'if I can't explain it, then I don't call it.'* I would suggest that when it comes to free-throw violations, you understand them enough to confidently rule on them.

Here are some key fundamentals to keep in your head for NFHS contests:

- Restrictions for all players apply until the ball touches the ring or backboard (NFHS) vs. release (NCAA).
- The first (or only) violation by the offense causes the ball to become dead immediately.
- If the violation is by the free thrower's opponent and the try is successful ... then ignore it. If unsuccessful you should have ruled a delayed dead ball and award a substitute free throw.
- If there is a SIMULTANEOUS violation (by each team), the ball is dead. No points can be scored and award the remaining free throws (if any). Or if none, then play is resumed by the team entitled to the AP Arrow.

Here's the one that makes it easier to administer. If the first violation is by the free thrower's opponent, then followed by a second violation by the free-thrower (or team mate) then you can IGNORE the 2nd violation, provided both offenders are in marked lane spaces.

If the 2nd violation is by the free thrower or someone behind the free-throw line extended and the 3pt arc, then penalize both.

Take special notice in your next game and critically evaluate your performance around judging and ruling on free throw violations.

Rule References
NFHS 9-1-3 and 4; 7-5-2c, NCAA 9.1

Knowledge Check

A-1 is fouled as time expires to end the fourth quarter of a tied game.

Shall the officials grant Team B's request to line up in their designated lane spaces?

No. (NFHS 8-6)

Coaching During a Timeout
by Tim Malloy

When a team is granted a timeout, the coaches, players and bench personnel are 'restricted' to a designated timeout area inside an imaginary rectangle near their bench and are not permitted to go beyond this area to provide more detailed instruction.

Now you don't want to be an official that "majors in the minor" and starts nitpicking about teams being out of their imaginary corral while standing during a 30-second timeout. Rather the point of this 60 Second tip is to know where a coach is legally permitted to be during a timeout so that he/she does not gain an unfair teaching advantage...

And where the coach is not allowed to be, is under the basket instructing front line players, or at the top of the key reviewing strategies with back court players.

For NFHS and NCAA play, the timeout area is formed by the boundaries of the sideline (including their bench), the end line, and an imaginary line extended from the free throw lane line closest to the bench area, and intersecting with an imaginary line extended from the coaching box line.

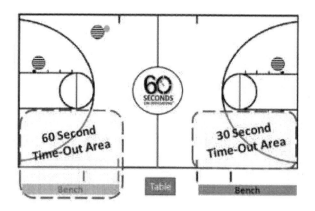

Quite often in crowded gyms where a visiting team may have to contend with boisterous home spectators sitting behind them, you will see a coach pull their team away from the bench area in order to communicate more effectively. However they must stay within the confines of the imaginary timeout rectangle.

So, keep in mind the time for on-court teaching and coaching is at practice. During an in-game timeout, all instruction must be done in the timeout area rectangle.

Rule References
NFHS: 1-13; NCAA 5-13-2

Knowledge Check

During a timeout, is a coach permitted to step into the lane area and demonstrate a low post move to his / her players?

No. (NFHS 1-13)

Going by the Book
by Tim Malloy

I t would seem to be a fair statement to say that every (high school) official with at least a few games under his or her belt has experienced the chill of being called to the table during a dead ball by the time keeper or the person handling the score book.

As you make the walk to the table you can see the table crew has that, *"it's not my fault"* expression on their faces.

"Take a deep breath and relax."

It's our fervent belief that rule competency breeds calmness and confidence in chaos. So if you digest this **"60 Second"** serving on the correct way to administer problems related to the score book, you will not be unduly stressed about what you may be presented with when you get to the table.

Just remember when dealing with the official score book you want to avoid being sidetracked by any explanation about "why" the player is not listed in the book.

By NFHS rules you WOULD assess an Administrative Technical Foul:
- To add a name and number to the team member list.
- To change the number of a player who is in the game or attempting to enter the game.

Again for NFHS, you would NOT assess an Administrative Technical Foul:

- If a player sitting on the bench is not listed in the official book.
- And there is no attempt to enter the game by the reserve player.
- Therefore, no technical foul.

Administrative Technical Fouls are:
- Charged to the team.
- Count towards the bonus.
- NOT charged to the player or indirectly to the coach.

So, if the scorer informs you that new player A-6 attempting to enter the game is not listed in the book, Team A would be charged with an Administrative Technical foul.

However, if A-6 were to somehow enter and leave the game before the bookkeeping error is discovered, there would be no penalty. The infraction must be penalized **when it occurs**.

Therefore, if the coach of Team A asks the table to enter A-7's number into the book during a timeout, the Administrative Technical Foul would be charged when the official scorekeeper enters A-7 into the book and notifies one of the officials.

Let's back up and review a couple of pre-game scenarios:

If before the game, but after the 10-minute mark, Team A's coach enters a player or players into the book, **ONE** Administrative Technical Foul is assessed. The game would begin with Team B attempting two free throws and inbound the ball at the division line.

As an aside, once the game is underway and the scorer states that No. 10 was the designated starter for Team A, but No. 20 started in his/her place, there is no Administrative Technical Foul. This infraction must be noticed before the ball becomes live to start the game.

While Administrative Technical Fouls have been greatly condensed to eliminate the parade of free throws for multiple bookkeeping mistakes, it is important to note the distinction between what happens in the pre-game **BEFORE** and **AFTER** the 10-minute mark.

A team's failure to provide its roster and starting lineup at least 10-minutes **BEFORE** the tip-off results in **ONE** Administrative Technical foul being charged to the offending team.

Any changes made **AFTER** the 10-minute mark would also be a maximum of **ONE** Technical foul charged to the offending team.

Knowing how to correctly administer any bookkeeping errors will make for a stress-free stroll to the scorer's table in all of your future games.

Rule References
NFHS 3-2-2b   10-1-1-2a,b,c

The 'Ability' to be a Valued Referee
by Tim Malloy

Our peer evaluations and coaches ratings all say you certainly have the ability to manage a basketball game, yet your schedule doesn't reflect this assessment.

The feedback you've been receiving at off-season camps and clinics is that you have the ability to rise to great heights as an official, but your assignor doesn't seem to share these sentiments.

So what gives?

The problem may be that while your on-court ability to inspire confidence with partners, coaches, and clinicians is impressive, your off-court ability does little to impress your assignor.

While you won't be able to rise up the officiating ladder without consistent and credible on-court abilty; your assignor is also grading you on your **AVAIL**-ability and **DEPEND**-ability.

No one would suggest you put your officiating avocation ahead of your family and work responsibilities; but the reality is your assignor has an obligation to the schools and leagues he or she covers, and if your **RELI**-ability is not something they can consistently count on, then your schedule will no doubt reflect that fact.

So if you want to move up on your assignor's depth chart, you might consider:

- Lightening your work schedule and commitments during the season, when possible, on the heavier game nights, and shifting these duties to off-nights.
- If you're involved with your child's extra-curricular activities, offer to take a supporting or assistant coaches role that might allow you more flexibility to handle your officiating responsibilities.
- If car problems have caused you to miss more than one game assignment, you might want to invest in a more dependable form of transportation. The potential to take on more game assignments with better wheels could likely cover the added monthly car payments.

It is commendable you're willing to put in the extra work to be a valued official in the eyes of coaches, outside observers, and by your peers. Just make sure you take the necessary steps to inspire the same confidence from your assignor.

Wide Eyes in a Three Person Crew
by Billy Martin

Following the trend of the NCAA, many scholastic (NFHS) conferences across America have been slowly transitioning to provide Three Person Officiating crews for most (or all) of their varsity level contests. This exciting trend provides better court coverage from a referee's perspective and statistically does

not impact the game from the number of whistles or types of rulings measured.

Most importantly it provides a wider opportunity for newer officials to gain experience at the varsity level and increases the number of available assignments throughout the regular season.

However this presents several new challenges. There is a higher burden on officiating associations (NFHS / IAABO / etc.) to train officials properly in working both Three Person and Two Person systems.

In states (or conferences) where both crews are utilized throughout the season, many veteran officials are bouncing back-and-forth between Two-Person and Three-Person.

Officials that work NCAA ball primarily, become unfamiliar with Two-Person mechanics and struggle to adjust if called upon to do such games.

As the complexities and differences between the two systems vary ... there are several "best practices" that can be adopted to minimize the "bounce" effect of jumping between the two styles of officiating.

 Leveraging these suggestions will make your transitions smoother and ratchet up your confidence when called upon to work a Three-Person game in your area.

Move More (than you think) in the Lead
When working a Three-Person Crew one of the most visible poor practices can be **not** rotating during a live ball - when you should. Officials that are primarily used to working two person crews know the value of minimizing their crossing of the lane. However in a game of three, it's imperative to think about rotating more often than not. It's easier to think about when not to rotate -- as compared to when you should.

Best Practice
As the lead official mentally prepare yourself to rotate every time down floor - and look for the opening to make it happen. Think to yourself ... "should I be going" ... "am I on the strong side" ... "am I in a good position."

By actually thinking about rotating **more**, you will most likely wind up rotating appropriately and can certainly ratchet it back as you adjust to the flow of the game.

Wide Eyes from the Outside
Possibly from the desire to focus so intently on their primary coverage area, many officials unfamiliar with Three-Person officiating get visually "locked-in" to their area and they fail to realize there is a live ball rotation occurring around them. This happens when

the lead makes a proper rotation and the outside officials fail to recognize the move. As a result the crew is totally off balance, the triangle is broken and a quick transition on a turnover may cause two officials in one spot.

Best Practice

When working from the outside (Trail / Center) make a dedicated effort to "keep your eyes attentive and wide open." Try actually (physically) opening your eyes "more-wide" and increasing your field of vision. If you are too relaxed from the outside and focusing in too small of an area ... your field of vision will tend to "close down."

Concentrate to keep "opening" pressure on your eyes by lifting your eyebrows and eyelids to create a larger opening.

Reading this may sound funny ...but that's how I describe the feeling of opening up your vision, similar to opening the aperture of a camera up wider, which allows more light into the picture.

Do the same with your eyes and you will see the game in a whole new light.

Be Uncomfortable in the Center Position

This recommendation refers to the feeling an official should get when the ball comes toward their side while working in the Center spot. Because the strong side should mainly be officiated by the Trail and Lead ... whenever the ball swings over to the Center's side, it should make them **feel uncomfortable - being alone** (over there) with the players, ball, and just themselves. Having ball pressure directly in front of the Center provides a very close proximity to the play and difficulty in getting really good depth perception.

Best Practice

When the ball gets too close to you as the Center official ... you should be thinking of moving to a better position. Most likely if the ball settles over on the C's side, the Lead referee should be initiating the live-ball rotation. When that ball comes over - take a slight glance up and "feel" your partner (the lead) starting to rotate. However, remember not to move too quickly.

Be patient and let the rotation occur with the lead moving first ... the opposite Trail moving to the new Center position, following by you moving backward into the new Trail spot. As always, the Center can move down or back to gain a better viewing angle of a play prior to any rotation occurring.

In conclusion, officials that bounce back and forth between Two-Person and Three-Person crews should focus on the key elements of "movement during live ball situations. Many times organizations focus on where officials should go during a dead ball, after foul reporting, switching, time-outs, etc, which are all important.

However, concentrating on movement as a crew to actually "officiate" the live play will make you a better referee and more comfortable as you jump back and forth during the scholastic season.

Preemptive Strikes to
Avoid the Fight

by Tim Malloy

Now good people can have an honest disagreement about the root causes for the uptick in the overall incivility emanating from spectators; but with the benefit of time and

perspective, most officials would likely agree it is a problem best dealt with by someone other than the working game officials.

This chapter will offer some advice for your consideration on how to preempt an ugly incident between players from erupting in your game.

Basketball officials, who have been in the middle of an ugly in-game episode, would likely share the same pose-event assessment of a snow skier surviving an avalanche:

> *"Everything was going along fine until I was upside down."*

Following are a few strategies to consider as preemptive measures to avoid an ugly game incident that could lead to hours of second-guessing, as well as unnecessary post-game paperwork and conversations with your assignor.

Not to mention the possibility of personal injury and legal action against you.

You won't find these tips in any manual, and you won't ever be able to prove they got you through a tough game without any problems, but if the price to you is a bit more focus and a little more hustle, wouldn't it be worth it?

Don't Wear Ignorance as a Badge of Honor

Being clueless to key factors involving the game you are about to officiate does not increase your ability to be objective. You need to know if there was any problems when they two team played last.

- Is there bad blood between the two schools or coaches?
- Does one team play very aggressive; maybe even a bit thuggish? (We've all seen video examples on YOU TUBE!)

Identify the Problem Child

Don't let one player with a bad attitude, or displaying an overly physical presence meant to intimidate, ruin your game.

If a team senses they are on their own in dealing with an overly physical opponent, they will undoubtedly take matters into their own hands.

Don't let one player negatively alter the play of the other nine players on the floor. There will be ample opportunities to call the appropriate fouls or violations on the "problem child" that might improve his conduct, or cause the coach to remove him/her from the game.

Either way, the problem has been solved and your game is back on track.

Referee like You're in the Stands

Consider the clarity you seem to have while watching a game in-person or on TV, and bring it into every contest you officiate.

Wouldn't it be great to be able to bring that same perspective and insight into every game we work, that we seem to enjoy from the comfort of the stands or our sofa?

If you can channel this "outside-in" mentality, you will be much better at noticing any change in the temperament of your game and be able to make the necessary adjustments.

Let the Ball Roll

Don't worry about tracking down the basketball during a dead ball. Your responsibility is to monitor the ten players on the court.

Someone will usually toss the ball back onto the court, or it will come to rest along one of the four walls that you can retrieve while still watching the players on the court.

Now if this seems a bit paranoid to you; I would pose you consider what you will do when you are alerted to fight/shoving match on the floor while you have your back to the court (or are crawling under the stands) chasing down the errant basketball. Let it roll!

Butter 'Em Up

While I'm not suggesting that you have to kiss anyone's backside; it may prove helpful to be a little empathetic to the plight of your players and coaches.

- Consider lending a helping hand to a fallen player.
- Offer a discreet "*good hustle*" compliment to two players involved in a jump ball.
- Get in quick to a jump ball scrum to keep tempers from flaring.
- Offer a sincere, but discreet "*tough night; keep hustling*" comment to a player on the bad end of a lopsided game.
- Coming out of a timeout, consider offering a discreet "*protect yourself*" comment to an assistant coach or a high-flying player whose team is pouring it on the opposition. You can call a foul; but that won't fix a player's broken wrist if they get low-bridged.

It doesn't cost anything to be nice, and it may save you some aggravation before the final horn sounds.

I hope you will accept these preemptive suggestions in the spirit they are offered, and that you leverage these ideas in a future game.

Handling the Block-Charge (a.k.a. Blarge)
by Tim Malloy & Billy Martin

The gym is packed and the fiercely competitive game is in the closing minutes when a player drives hard to the basket. There is a collision in the lane and you blow your whistle and **quickly signal a player control foul**.

Out of the corner of your eye you see your **partner signaling for a block**.

Now what?

Let's add the **block-charge**, or **"blarge"** as it's sometimes called, to the list of what to talk about in any scholastic or collegiate pregame discussion. But also, let's know how to correctly administer this sticky situation should it happen to you, and we'll also offer a tip on how steer clear of this officiating nightmare.

Let's play it out:

- A-1 drives to the basket and releases the ball while in the air.
- Contact occurs between shooter A-1 and defender B-1 while the ball is in the air ...
- ... and before A-1 returns to the floor.
- The ball goes in the basket.

Two whistles blow and two different preliminary signals are given on the play.

At this point, preventative maintenance is out the window, so administering the play correctly is the only thing that won't compound the problem.

While airborne A-1 committed a **charging foul**;

- It **is not** a **player control foul** ...
- because the two fouls result in a **double personal foul**.

The double foul **does not** cause the ball to become dead on the field goal attempt and therefore the officials **score the goal**.

Play is resumed at the **point of interruption**, which is a throw-in by Team B anywhere along the end line.

If the **ball had not gone in** the basket, we would have resumed play with the **alternating possession arrow** because there is no team control on a try for goal.

So the lesson to be learned here is ...

- Talk about this **EXACT situation** in your pre-game conference, so you are ready for it.
- Give **NO preliminary signals** from the outside (**TRAIL or CENTER**)
- If you have a **double whistle** with no preliminary signals ... gain eye contact with your partner as you decide who should take the play.
- In a two person crew (all levels) it typically will go to the **LEAD** as the play is coming toward them, in the lane area.

- In a three person crew, **mechanics differ** on the level. While **NFHS/IAABO** mechanics still **allow the CENTER** to officiate their half of the lane ... and **CCA** mechanics encourage the **LEAD** to take all block-charges in the restricted lane area.
- NCAA officials must also consider **secondary defenders** under the basket (see below).
- Regardless of the level, it is imperative to **talk about this in pre-game** to agree on **WHO** takes that call and what to do in a double whistle situation.
- If you do have a **true double foul (block / charge)** with preliminary signals given ... just administer it properly and move on to the point of interruption or the alternating possession arrow, which ever applies.

NCAA officials have more information to process when dealing with a potential block / charge in the restricted lane area. For **NCAA only**, a secondary defender may not establish initial legal guarding position under the basket when playing a player who is in control of the ball (i.e., dribbling or shooting) or who has released the ball for a pass or try for goal.

A secondary defender is a teammate who has helped a primary defender who has been beaten by an opponent because he failed to establish or maintain a guarding position. "Under the basket" is defined as from the front and side of the ring to the front of the backboard. A player is considered under the basket when any part of either foot is in this area. A player straddling this marked area is considered to be under the basket.

College players while establishing position in any outnumbering fast break situation, may not establish initial legal guarding position under the basket since there is no primary defender. When illegal contact occurs, such contact shall be called a blocking foul, unless the contact is intentional or flagrant.

At any level you officiate, the key is to talk about this situation in pre-game and make sure the crew is on the same page if a double whistle occurs.

Rule References
NFHS 4-19-8; NCAA 4.35.7, 10.15.g

Knowledge Check

On a double whistle "Blarge" situation, you must decide what happened first while the less experienced official defers their ruling to that of the senior referee.

True or False?

False.
Both fouls are recorded and administered accordingly.

Dealing with Abusive Fans
by Billy Martin

Having an opportunity to observe a high school basketball game (on a rare night off) I found myself amazed at the very aggressive attitude and behavior of adults in the stands, directed toward players AND officials.

So you're saying ... *"where have you been the last 20 years?"* Well, I guess at some point you finally realize that enough is enough.

While state associations, local conferences, and rule governing bodies have implemented policies and procedures to deal with unruly fans, it seems as though (in general and overall) a crowd can be very difficult to keep in control as compared to the players on the court, regardless of what guidelines you put in place.

The following offer some situations and the best practices designed to keep an overzealous fan base from crossing over the line of proper decorum.

> **"It may be time for us ALL to step up our enforcement on abusive fans."**

NFHS Rule 2-8-1, Official's Additional Duties, provide the following guideline to address unsporting conduct by a player, coach, substitute, team attendant, or follower.

- **Home management** (or game committee) is responsible for **spectator** behavior.
- **Reasonable** control is expected.
- Officials **may** rule (key words, **MAY RULE**) technical fouls on either **team** if its spectators "**interfere** with the **proper conduct** of the game."
- **Discretion** must be used when ruling such a technical foul.
- Teams should not be **unjustly punished** (either side) for ruling a foul, or lack of ruling.

The following are recommended procedures (via NFHS) Rules Committee if team supporters become **unruly** or **interfere** with the game:

- **STOP** the game.
- Request **HOST MANAGEMENT** to resolve the situation.
- Do **NOT RESUME** the game until management has resolved (or is resolving) the situation and game can resume in an orderly manner.
- Keep player **SAFETY** (and your crew's safety) as the key concern at all times.

Here are some key best practices to consider prior and during each game.

- Identify (and remember) **who** is the designated school **representative** that will be present if problems occur.
- If no representative is available, the **head coach** will serve as host management.
- Never **address a fan** directly. Summon the school representative to deal with any issues.
- Always respond when a **fan's unsporting** comments, which are **directed at a player**,

start interfering with the game. Never let fans berate a player to the point it interrupts the game and the player reacts to such commentary. Use your calming techniques with the player and have administration deal with the fan directly and have them removed.

- If a **fan purposely interferes** with the game by blowing a whistle in the stands or running on the court to stop a fast break, make sure to penalize these acts (via a Technical Foul) and not place the offended team at a disadvantage.
- It is always a technical foul if the **head coach incites crowd reactions** by encouraging or suggesting fans to "gang up" on the officiating crew or the opposing team.
- Unsportsmanlike conduct from **administrative staff and other bench personnel** should never be tolerated - and can be dealt with directly by the referee by ruling a technical foul.

Keep in mind these items and hopefully you can deal with abusive fans in a professional manner to keep your game running smoothly.

Rule References
NFHS 2-8-1, 10-4-1

Knowledge Check

If you think you can humorously diffuse a situation involving an abusive spectator, it is an acceptable first-course of action?

No. Do not engage spectators. Inform the site manager.

Where to Spot the Ball

by Tim Malloy

A key part of "getting the play right" is where the ball is spotted after the official makes their ruling on a violation, a non-shooting foul or resumes play at the completion of a timeout.

This often overlooked component of the game can lead to careless spot placements, which will undoubtedly create unfair advantages for teams inbounding the ball.

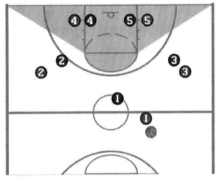

Be vigilant in visualizing your **"Inbound Triangle"** for determining throw in spots for non-shooting fouls in the offensive team's front court.

Did the foul occur **inside** your imaginary lines running from the free throw line elbows to the end line corners, or at the top of the key?

If so, the throw in spot will be on the **endline.**

If the foul took place **outside** the imaginary lines, then the spot throw in will take place on the **sideline.**

Careless ball placement, or a lack of understanding of the "Inbound triangle" will lead to several unfair advantages given (or missed opportunities for end line throw-ins) throughout the course of your game.

It is the location of the foul, not the location of where the ball is at the time of the foul that determines where the resumption of play throw in is to take place.

Conversely for timeouts, it is the location of the ball, not where the player or coach is who requests the stoppage in play that determines where the ball will be spotted to resume play.

The inconsistent spotting of throw-ins to resume play is common complaint of supervisors and those evaluating game tape. Be mindful of these throw in tips and you will be an "Image of Difference" official!

Knowledge Check

Where is the ball to be put in play after a double foul that occurred in the lane while A-1 is dribbling the ball above the free throw line extended?

For NFHS & NCAA the inbound will occur at the point of interruption which is where A-1 is dribbling the ball.(7-5-3b -NF; 7-5-5-NCAA.)

Throw-In Movement
by Tim Malloy

An important topic to review is what the player inbounding the ball may **or** may not do during a throw-in.

By way of review, the thrower may not be the first player to legally touch the ball they have put into play. Also they must be mindful of breaking the plane with the ball and creating a legal opportunity for the defense to steal it or cause a held ball ruling.

Let's look at the out-of-bounds movement of the player charged with the responsibility of throwing the ball in, and why an official's comment to, *"hold your spot"* is not a literal command.

The designated throw-in spot pointed out to a player is actually a...

- **three-foot WIDE area** and
- and there is **NO LIMIT on how far BACK** the player may step in order to complete the throw-in.

Since the traveling rule is not in effect (during a throw-in), the official need not pay attention to a pivot-foot. However, the thrower must keep at least **ONE FOOT** over the three-foot designated spot area until the ball is released.

While the important thing is to get the play right, keep in mind the mechanic to signal a violation of the designated spot throw-in is a downward pointed finger at the spot with a side-to-side waving motion.

*This infraction is **NOT** a TRAVELING VIOLATION and should not be signaled as such.*

Remember, when attempting to inbound the ball, the thrower...

- can legally step **ON** the **boundary line**.
- shall **NOT** step **over** the boundary line.
- may legally **jump** in the **air** to release the ball.

If the court does not provide ample access along the end lines and side lines for the throw-in, the official may direct the defender to step back enough to give the thrower at least three-feet of unobstructed space.

During a designated spot throw-in only the thrower may be out of bounds. However, after a made basket or an awarded goal the thrower is permitted to...

- run along the end line...
- and (optionally) pass the ball to teammate who is standing out of bounds (along the end line) to gain better access for completing the throw-in.

A timeout requested by the inbounding team does not forfeit their right to "run the end line" if they had the privilege prior to the timeout being granted. Good concentration (and a helpful partner) will eliminate any memory lapses as to the type of throw-in to be administered coming out of a break in the game action.

The numerous throw-ins during the course of play are all loaded with potential problems that can bring your game to a grinding halt and thrust you into the unwanted spotlight. Hopefully this *"60 Second"* snippet on throw-in movement will eliminate this unnecessary headache for you in all future games.

NFHS Reference: 4-42; 7-4-6; 9-2

Knowledge Check

A-1 is attempting a throw-in after a made basket by Team B when B-2 fouls A-2 near the inbound spot.

Team A is not in the bonus.

May Team A resume the throw-in anywhere along the end line, or is this a designated spot throw in?

*Team A **may run** the end line. It **is not** a designated spot throw-in as Team A does not lose the ability to run the end line if they choose. (NFHS 7.5.7.C)*

Who's Your Shooter?

by Tim Malloy

I f your officiating crew is focused in on the game at hand, a "wrong shooter" scenario will be quickly snuffed out before the fuse is lit and the suspect player is given the ball.

The calling official will have their shooter mentally locked in as they proceed from the reporting area to the foul line, and their partner will provide a safety net by pointing to the fouled player and temporarily committing the player's number to memory.

If the foul results in a trip to the other end of the court to shoot, a verbal notice by one of the non-calling officials in earshot of the players ("21, you're shooting.") will nip any subterfuge in the bud. And establishing a proper up tempo pace between the time of the foul and actually administering the free throws will go a long way to thwart any seeds of deceit being planted in your game.

However, if prevention escapes you and you are faced with this correctable error scenario, your only salvation is to extricate yourself the right way.

If the crew believes there is a reasonable explanation for the mix up, fix it and move on...

But if you feel there is no justification for this mix up (i.e. post player fouled; point guard steps to the line), you would be well within in the rules to administer a technical foul for unsportsmanlike conduct. Now a stern or wary glance at the offending player and in the direction of the offending coach may be the better course of action instead of a technical, but that penalty option is certainly at your disposal.

Now if a player (A-1) is injured or disqualified before they can attempt their free throws:

- A-1's replacement (A-6) will shoot **ALL** of A-1's free throws.
- Team A's coach **MAY NOT** substitute a player (A-7) to shoot the remaining free throws due to A-1 being fouled.
- A substitute thrower is permitted only if A-6 claimed to be injured after the first free throw, which is highly unlikely.

Free throws awarded for a technical foul (NFHS) may be shot by different players. Free throws awarded to a fouled player who is replaced because of injury must be shot by the substitute.

If a technical foul is called prior to the start of the game (on Team B) and the game will begin with Team A shooting free throws:

- Team A's coach **MAY REPLACE** a starter (A-5) with a bench player (A-6) to shoot the free throws.
- A-5 **MAY NOT** re-enter the game until after the clock has been properly started.

Prevention and discretion will serve you well should this wrong shooter subplot develop in your game; the key is to be armed with the knowledge to properly rule on it, if and when it occurs.

NFHS Rule References
2-10; 3-2; 3-3-4; 8-3; 10-3-6

It's All About Control
by Billy Martin

Team control affects many things within the ebb and flow of a game. Starting with the 2011-12 season the NFHS has changed the rule regarding team control to be in line with the NCAA which now includes **TEAM CONTROL** during a **THROW-IN**.

Consider the following situations where a **TEAM IS IN CONTROL** versus **NOT** in control.

Remember, player control (defined as holding or dribbling a live ball inbounds) is a component of team control and has different implications within the rules.

So what is **TEAM CONTROL?**

See the following chart on the next page to distinguish between when a team is IN control versus a team NOT in control.

Team IN Control	NO Team Control
During a Throw In (New NFHS 2011-12)	Ball is in Flight for a Try or Tap
Player Holding or Dribbling a Live Ball Inbounds**	Opponent Secures Control
Live Ball Passed Around by Teammates	Ball Becomes Dead
During an Interrupted Dribble	Jump Ball
During a Live / Loose Ball – the Last Team in Control	Touching of a Rebound

*denotes player control as well.

The following are just some of the areas influenced by team control:

BACK COURT VIOLATIONS

For a back-court violation to occur,
the team violating...

- Must have **CONTROL** of the ball...
- and must be the **LAST** to touch the ball in the front-court...
- and must be the **FIRST** to touch the ball in the back-court.

Team Control is one of the three ingredients of a back-court ruling.

FREE THROWS

Whenever a foul is committed by a member the team in control...

- A **team control** foul is ruled.
- **No** free-throws are awarded to the offended team.
- Team control fouls **do count** toward the team's bonus.

JUMP BALL

If a **re-jump** is required **before** team control is established:

- For **NFHS**, the re-jump must be administered between the **two players involved**.
- **NCAA** is different and allows **any two players** to jump.

THROW-INS

Starting back in 2011-12 season the NFHS considered a **TEAM to be in CONTROL** during a throw-in.

- This means there are no free throws awarded for common fouls committed by the team inbounding the ball while in the bonus.
- NCAA also recognizes team control during a throw-in.
- A team inbounding the ball is permitted to control the ball in the back-court without a violation as this rule does not affect backcourt, three second violations, traveling / dribbling, and the alternating-possession throw-in rules.

TRY FOR GOAL

Since there is **no team control** during a **try (or tap)**, any subsequent rulings that rely on knowing which team is in control are effected, such as:

- **Double Fouls (unsuccessful goal):** Since no team is in control during an unsuccessful try/tap, if a double foul occurs -- the point of interruption will be referring to the Alternating-Possession arrow to determine which team is awarded the ball.
- **Double Fouls (successful goal):** Point of Interruption is the made basket.
- **Ball Lodges between Basket/Backboard:** Again, no team control, refer to the A-P arrow to determine possession and continue play.
- After a try for goal and the ball deflects into the back-court, either team may control the ball without penalty.

LOOSE BALLS

While the ball remains loose, after a team was in control:

- It always remains in control of the **team last in control**...
- **Unless** it's a try/tap for goal, then no team control exists.

INTERRUPTED DRIBBLE

A loose ball is not the same thing as an interrupted dribble. A ball that "momentarily" gets away from a dribbler (in-control) of the ball, is still considered to be **IN CONTROL** of that team.

Also:

- The player (with an interrupted dribble) is considered to have lost control ... but the **TEAM is STILL** considered to be in control.
- A three second violation can be ruled (if appropriate) since the team is still in control during an interrupted dribble.

These are just a few of the many areas where team control determines how an official should rule on a particular play. Know the differences between control vs. no control and you will always be on the right side of the play.

Rule References
NFHS 4-12-1, 4-12-2, 4-12-6, 4-19-7, 4-8-2, 9-9,

Knowledge Check

The jump ball between A-1 and B-1 to start the game caroms to the sideline where it is simultaneously touched by A-2 and B-2 before going out of bounds.

How is the game resumed?

A-2 and B-2 will jump at the center circle.

Get the Fight Right
by Tim Malloy

In light of various reported high school and collegiate on-court fighting incidents, it reminds us that even the best officials can get caught in a nasty situation where your "paramedic officiating" training can come in handy.

That is to say, calm and instinctive responses that have been drilled into you and allow you to block out the noise of the on-court crisis to coolly restore order and correctly rule on what has transpired.

And there is arguably nothing more in need of this officiating skill set than when a fight breaks out in your game.

Why the skirmish occurred and how to possibly prevent one from happening are topics for another day. For now, let's take another **"60 Second"** look at the key components to consider so you may confidently and competently rule on a fight in a scholastic (**NFHS**) contest.

PLAYERS ON THE COURT

If an **equal** number of players from both teams participate in the fight...

- **All participants** are charged with flagrant technical fouls and disqualified.
- **No free throws** are awarded and the ball is in-bounded at the point of interruption.

If there is an **unequal** number of players who participate in the fight...

- **All participants** are charged with flagrant technical fouls and disqualified.
- The offended team will be awarded **two free throws** for **each additional player**.

Keep in mind; taunting may be viewed as the "first punch." If the provoked player physically retaliates, both players are charged with flagrant technical fouls and are disqualified.

PLAYERS ON THE BENCH

Simply stated, if a player leaves the bench area and comes onto the court during a skirmish, they are charged with a flagrant technical foul and disqualified.

Penalties for bench personnel stepping onto the court will also impact the head coach.

For those reserves that **ENTER** the court, but <u>**DO NOT**</u> participate in the fight...

- The head coach is charged with **maximum of one** indirect technical foul ...
- regardless of how many bench players come onto the floor.

If there is an <u>**equal**</u> number of non-fighting bench personnel on the court...

- Those players are disqualified.
- No free throws are awarded for their actions.

If there is an <u>**unequal**</u> number of players who leave the bench area and **do not** fight...

- Those players are disqualified.
- The offended team would be awarded a **maximum** of **two free throws** for this segment of the scenario.

For **Bench Personnel** who <u>**do**</u> **participate** in the fight...

- The heads coach is assessed an **indirect technical** foul for <u>**EACH**</u> bench person who participates.
- Remember, three indirect technical fouls would result in the head coach being disqualified.

If there is an **equal** number of bench personnel fighting on the court...

- **No free throws** are awarded for their actions and play would resume at the point of interruption.

If there is an **unequal** number of players who leave the bench area and participate in the fight:

- The offended team would be awarded two free throws for **each** additional player involved.
- Also the offended team would receive the ball at the division line for a throw-in.

For liability purposes, disqualified players are permitted to remain on the bench and should not to be ordered to leave the court area without proper adult supervision.

Now in the aftermath of a fight, typically no one comes away from the incident unscathed, and the officials will be at the front of the line to be evaluated, and maybe second-guessed.

The cries of *"Ref, let them play; you're not the game!"* and *"Ref, it's getting physical; somebody is going to get hurt!"* fit nicely onto a double-edge sword that may slice you when things go bad. Second-guessing is a spectator perk.

It's frightening to consider all of the hard, competitive plays that take place in a game where players simply pick themselves up and resume play without any retaliation. In hindsight we understand and shudder a bit knowing any one of these plays could be motivation enough to provoke a verbal or physical response that sets in motion the events outlined above.

That a fight happened is most likely out of your control; what is in your control is how quickly and calmly you extinguish the skirmish and correctly mete out the penalties according to NFHS rules.

Hopefully this "60 Seconds" session on fighting has bolstered your *'paramedic training'* in this vital area.

Rule References
NFHS 4-18; 10-4; 10-6

Knowledge Check

A-1 dunks over B-1 and then taunts B-1.

B-1 retaliates and punches A-1.

You blow your whistle and….??

Both players are charged with flagrant technical fouls and both are disqualified. A-1's taunting action is considered, "the first punch" so they both are ejected. (NFHS 4.18.2)

The Lowdown on Inbounds Plays
by Billy Martin

The throw-in is one of three methods of making a dead ball become live, along with the jump ball and free throw.

Normally these events take place without significant consequence or violations, however, every now and then a play crops up that looks "so strange" it makes you double-take.

Here are three (**NFHS**) throw-in situations you might see in a future high school game that you will be better prepared to rule on correctly.

Play #1: Team A is inbounding under their own basket. A-1, in an attempt to throw the ball to A-3 all the way back into their backcourt, tosses the ball and it caroms off the side of Team A's backboard falling to the floor directly in front of A-1.

A-1 steps inbounds with both feet touching the floor and picks up the ball and passes to A-5.

Is this a legal play??

No, this play is **NOT LEGAL**.

- The player throwing the ball inbounds may **not** be the **first to touch** the ball on the court. This is a violation.
- The ball remained live, as it caromed off the side of the back-board but one of the other 9 players on the court would need to touch (or be touched) by the ball for this play to be legal.

Play #2: Thrower-in A-1 tosses the inbounds pass off the leg of B-1 whose back is turned away from the play. A-1 steps onto the court, secures the ball and dribbles to the basket for an easy lay-up.

Is this play legal?

Yes, this is a **LEGAL** play.

- Since the ball touched B-1's leg, the thrower is permitted to gain possession of the ball.
- As B-1 did not intentionally kick the ball, the official should allow this play to continue.

Play #3: A-1 inadvertently holds the ball across the end-line plane during the throw-in. B-1 who is guarding the inbounds pass, instinctively **grabs the ball** so firmly that A-1 cannot pull the ball back.

The official penalized B-1 with a **TECHNICAL FOUL** for delay of game.

Is the official correct?

No, the official is **not** correct here.

This is considered a **held ball**.

- Since the ball is being held across the end-line plane by A-1, the defender (B-1) may reach for the ball within the rules, provided B-1 does not reach through the plane.
- Additionally, once the ball is considered "held" by both players, the official would rule an **alternating possession** throw-in. If the initial throw-in by A-1 was the result of an AP arrow ruling, Team A would again be awarded possession because the AP throw-in had not been completed. The AP throw-in ends when the ball is legally touched by a player who is inbounds, or the throw-in team commits a violation.
- Remember, there is team control during a throw-in for both NFHS and NCAA games which brings consistency to the enforcement of fouls committed by the inbounding team.

Hopefully, this quick three play refresher will keep you on the correct side of any unusual ball-inbounding scenarios.

NFHS References 6-4-4; 7-6-4; 9-2-7

Grasping the Ring
by Tim Malloy

Nothing will bring a coach or a group of spectators to their feet faster than an opposing player grabbing a fistful of the rim during a hotly contested play.

"Grasping the Ring" is the correct technical term, and a Technical Foul is sometimes (but not always) charged to the offending player for this action.

The sight and sound of the ring being pulled down and snapped back into position during a live ball will no doubt get your attention, and that of everyone in the gym, so let's take sixty seconds to review a few scenarios that will allow you to confidently and competently make the correct ruling on if a whistle is needed rule on **basket interference** and/or issue a **technical foul**.

Whether the player doing the grasping is on offense or defense, the basis for the rulings are the same. But for this scenario the perpetrator is on the team with the ball:

> A-2 leaps in the air to follow up A-1's missed shot. A-2 mis-times his leap for a put-back dunk and grasps the ring. A-2 momentarily hangs on the basket before releasing his grip and returning to the floor.

Now you need to quickly **locate the ball** and review the play in your mind to determine if the ball is:

Outside the Cylinder
Inside the Cylinder
On or In the Basket

- **OUTSIDE** the cylinder --
  No whistle is needed. Let the **play continue**.
- **INSIDE** the cylinder --
  No whistle needed. Let the play continue. However, if the player causes the movable ring to collapse and when it snaps back and makes contact with the ball, blow your whistle and rule **basket interference**.
- **ON or IN the BASKET** -- Blow your whistle and rule **basket interference**.

The merits for charging A-2 with a Technical Foul for hanging on the basket are a separate issue and can be answered with one question:

Was it done to prevent injury?

The suggestion here is to err on the side of caution and not be too hasty in hitting A-2 with a "T."

Consider A-2's ability to safely return to the floor without causing injury to himself (his legs swinging outward) or any player around him (landing on top of another player).

A "chin-up" or "pull-up" by A-2 or a fancy "dismount" will likely draw a cheer from the crowd and give you an extra split-second to mentally review the play and charge A-2 with a technical foul if warranted.

"It's better to be late and right, than early and wrong."

And like the Superior Court judge who stated, "*I can't describe it, but I know it when I see it,*" when asked the difference between nude photos and pornography; so too is it with players hanging on the basket. When you see it, you will know which one's warrant a Technical Foul.

So, filter out the chaos of the coaches and the crowd and the snapping sound of the bending basket to identify the location of the ball at the time of the incident. Make your decision to blow or not blow your whistle based on this information.

Assess if the hanging on the basket warrants a Technical Foul. If in your judgment it is obvious the player was in control of his body and his actions were for show and not safety and it **must** be penalized, then blow your whistle. If you're not 100% sure, hold your whistle.

If you follow these tips you will no doubt grab the brass ring on plays involving grasping the ring.

Reference NFHS Rules: 4-6-1-4; 10-3-3

Knowledge Check

A-1 loses his balance while shooting and grabs the rim to prevent an injury -- and comes in contact with the ball -- while it is on the rim. Is this a legal play?

No, it is basket interference on A-1.

Learning from Observations
by Billy Martin

As we all strive to become better at the craft of officiating, sometimes we forget very simple things that contribute to our success on the court.

As former Supervisor of Officials for IAABO Camden, NJ (Board #34) I've had the opportunity to observe and evaluate several hundred scholastic officials over the course of several years all with varying degrees of proficiency and skill levels.

Below is a short list of "common" observed items that appear on our rating forms as **areas of needed improvement.** I characterize all of these as "simple fixes" and small changes that can lead to major improvements in everyone's game.

Would any of the following appear on
YOUR evaluation sheet?

Problem #1:
Spot of Foul Mechanics / Signals

As the NFHS Official manual suggests (Section 2.4.2) - "It is imperative that a definite procedure in officiating mechanics be used when a foul occurs." The manual goes on to list the duties (and order) that should be done by the calling official.

From my observations, 80% of the time the calling official **DOES NOT** (but should):

- **Verbally inform** the player that he/she has fouled - stating jersey **color and jersey number.**
- Lower the (closed fist) foul signal and indicate the nature of the foul by giving a **preliminary signal** at the spot of the foul.

Many times the official stops the clock correctly (whistle with closed fist raised) but then proceeds directly toward the reporting zone without finishing the appropriate signals and mechanics at the spot.

Recommendation

Get in front of a **mirror and practice** with the official's manual open. Make sure you know the exact procedure and signals for the spot of any foul as well as the reporting zone - which are two distinct items.

Make sure you take the time and deploy the proper spot of foul mechanics, each and every time, as appropriate.

Problem #2:
Staying with Perimeter Shooters

One of the hardest **bad habits** to break as a novice official is the desire to **"follow the ball"** versus keeping a focus on your primary coverage area (PCA). This tendency carries over to shooters as well.

When it comes to perimeter shooters (on the wing) in the corners, or anywhere on the court, less experienced officials (by my observation) tend to:

- Turn their head (and attention) **away** from the perimeter shooter – **well before** the play is completed.
- **Follow the ball** flight - instead of watching the defender and airborne shooter until the play is completely over.
- **Miss illegal contact** after the play is completed ... sometimes even borderline intentional / flagrant contact.

It is extremely important to break the habit of following the ball flight and **"stay with your shooters"** until the play is completely over. Trust your partner(s) to watch the other players on the floor and remain focused in your primary coverage area (PCA).

Recommendation

Use a "**mental cue**" when watching the play. In your mind, say something like - "**stay**" , to remind you to stay with that shooter until the play is over. Or maybe mentally count - "**one-one-thousand**" before even thinking about turning your head away from the play. The key is to remain focused on the shooter until you are confident the play is completed.

Observation #3:
The Need to Develop a Patient Whistle

The skill of creating a "**space in time**" between an official's signal (whistle) and the actual violation or foul occurring is a key best practice for all referees to learn.

Often I observe an official **"blowing the whistle"** at the **exact time** a foul is happening. Much of the time the official is moving to get into position or in transition - and not in a relaxed position.

Problems with this include:

- Anticipation causes the official **to blow the whistle** early.
- Sometimes the play turns out different than anticipated ... and you are **stuck** with the ruling now.
- There is no turning back now.

Experienced officials develop a "knack" for allowing a tiny fraction of a second to mentally evaluate the play **before signaling** with their whistle. This permits time to allow the play to continue without interruption on the official's part keeping the game moving and ruling properly on the play.

Recommendation

Loosen the grip on the whistle with your mouth. Whenever possible you should have a relaxed grip on the whistle so there is time needed to load the whistle with air. That split second can make the difference between an official with a perceived "tight/impatient" whistle, or a relaxed one. It's permissible to **anticipate the play** but don't **anticipate the ruling**.

Hopefully none of these observations appear on your ratings sheets. If they do work try working on incorporating some of these recommendations to see major improvement in your game.

Resolutions for Every New Season
by Al Battista

Consider incorporating some of these successful habits into your game for the beginning of every new officiating season.

Keep **your written list** handy and review it often to make sure you are sticking to your own personal resolutions.

Resolution Ideas for Top Officials

1. Be at every game **on time** and be prepared to officiate.
   Are you allowing enough travel time to get to your contest? Early and relaxed is better than stressed and late.

2. Do your **homework** preparation before each game.
   Are you aware of the records, history, or match-ups that exist between the two teams you're officiating?

3. Have a thorough **pre-game**.
   If you are the referee, you should be leading the conversation. In absence of a strong crew leader ... take control and drive a good, conversational pre-game covering as many topics as time will allow.

4. Have a beneficial **post-game** without "nitpicking" each other.
   It's always easy to start this conversation by asking the question, "is there anything we could have done better out there tonight."

5. Master the **rules** and know the intent of the rules.
   When is the last time you had your "nose" in the rule (or case) book? Take one hour per week and curl up with your favorite rule topic that gives you troubles. A great reference is "Beyond the Rules" – visit **www.gobeyondtherules.com** *for more info.*

6. Enforce "**freedom** of **movement**."
   Review NFHS 4-24 as it relates to legal and illegal use of the hands/arms. Know when to enforce illegal contact inhibiting a player's freedom to move.

7. Have excellent **clock management** skills.
   Are you keenly aware of the clock at all times? This is a good item to practice at all levels - maintaining "definite knowledge" of time remaining after stoppages.

8. **Communicate** more with your partner(s).
   Are you maintaining good "eye contact" with your partners at all times? Do you verbalize clearly at the spot of the foul (or violation). Make sure to drop the whistle and sell rulings that need selling - loud enough to be heard by all.

9. Know which team(s) are in the **bonus** and double bonus.
   There is no excuse for a crew having to correct this error. Keep an eye on scoreboard as the penalty approaches.

10. Know how many **fouls** a team can "**give**."
    When its crunch time and you know a team will be fouling their opponent... be aware of how many it takes before they shoot the bonus.

11. Know the **team control** rule.
    It is fundamental to the game and can be applied in many situations.

12. Penalize **unsportsmanlike conduct** on players and coaches.
    Talk about this in your pre-game conferences and be prepared to enforce proper decorum. Remember however, once a player/coach is ejected there is no turning back or changing your mind.

13. Be a good **partner**.
    Avoid speaking negatively to a coach/player about one of your partner's rulings. Despite any notion to the contrary, the only friend you have on the court are your partners. You ultimately rise and fall as one, so support each other 100%.

14. Be a good **mentor**.
    Offer constructive advice to less experienced officials at every opportunity. Take a moment to consider how fond you are to this day of the officials who made time to help your game and your career. Be one of those officials.

15. Officiate **every possession** hard.
    Think officiating in chunks of "2 minutes" at a time and never take a break on a possession. Work hard and be in the right spot to make the proper ruling - "every time."

16. **Break down video** once or twice a week.
    Ask the school for a copy of game video and review it with a critical eye. It's amazing what you will learn about your game. You will begin to officiate with the goal to, "beat the tape."

17. **Observe games** and be positive.
    If you are sitting in the stands watching your peers, be positive and never criticize a colleague in front of others. Discuss plays and mechanics in private remembering to offer constructive advice.

18. Watch your **diet**.
    The new season is always a good time to reset your caloric intake and keep your body running efficiently for the long haul ahead.

19. Have an in-season **exercise program**.
    If the only exercise you get is on the court during a game, you're exposing yourself to potential injury or worse. Incorporate stretching, strengthening, and aerobic exercise as a weekly routine.

20. Get proper **rest** between games and do not overwork.
    Muscles and joints need a break to recover properly so make sure to give it to them. If you're driven by the money or prestige of a heavy schedule, consider that you could lose both due to an injury brought on by overtaxing your body.

As the year unfolds we encourage you to learn and grow from each game. Build upon last season's successes and mistakes, and always strive to become a better official each and every time you walk onto the court. The game of basketball and the student-athletes deserve that.

Be Technically Correct
by Tim Malloy

T he sound of the horn and the official's whistle are heard to end an uneventful first half of play in an NFHS contest.

However, while the players are **still on the court and before the teams have left their benches** heading to their respective locker rooms for halftime, an official blows their whistle and rules an unsportsmanlike technical foul on A-1.

After the foul is reported, the officiating crew allows B-6, who was **NOT** in the game when the second quarter ended, to shoot the free throws for the technical foul **BEFORE** the players retire to the locker room.

Let's break down the administration of this scenario.

> **Should the officials administer the technical foul free throws while all the players are still on the court at the end of the first half?**

The answer is simply, **NO**.

The free throws for the technical foul are administered as part of the **third quarter**, to start the 2nd half – which occurs **after the halftime intermission**.

The officials should meet before leaving the court, away from the players and coaches, to discuss the play and then report the information to the score table.

Can B-6 or a player not on the court at the time of the infraction shoot the free throws for the technical foul?

> **YES**.   Any player or bench personnel is permitted to shoot the free throws for a technical foul.
>
> During an intermission **all** team members are considered **bench personnel**. Since this technical foul occurred **after** the horn to end the 2nd quarter, **A-1 is considered to be bench personnel**.

Remember:

- The technical foul charged to A-1 counts toward the team foul total (bonus) in the **second half**.
- The technical foul charged to A-1 counts towards A-1's **personal foul total** for disqualification.
- Because the technical foul was assessed to a bench person, the head coach of Team A would also be assessed an **indirect technical** and would lose the coaching box

privilege (if used) and must remain seated for the second half.

- The Referee should switch the alternating possession arrow as normal procedure to end the first half before retiring to the locker room.

The Second Half would begin with:

- Team B shooting two free throws.
- Team B being awarded the ball at the division line to start the 3rd quarter.
- Team B's throw-in is the result of the technical foul and not the alternating-possession arrow, and the **AP arrow would not change** to start the third quarter.

In the blink of an eye, an uneventful game can be splattered with drama so be prepared to rules confidently and competently if the above scenario unfolds before you.

NFHS Rule Reference: 10-4; 10-5

Knowledge Check

A technical foul is ruled on a player or coach after the horn ending the first half and before the teams head to their respective locker rooms.

Do you shoot the free throws prior to the intermission since the players are still on court <u>or</u> afterward when they return from the locker room?

The officials would begin the second half by shooting the free-throws for the technical foul.

Jump to a Good Start in Every Game
by Tim Malloy

For our basketball officiating purposes, we will modify the *'one chance to make a good first impression'* adage to include having only one chance to make a good toss in a regulation game so it is important to get it right the first time.

Any miscue surrounding the opening jump ball can undermine a crew's credibility and go beyond the embarrassment of the opening minute mistake.

We offer the following checkpoints to help keep you out of harm's way in the game's opening moments.

Face the Proper Direction -- Nothing can get the train off the tracks faster than having a player score at the wrong basket off of the opening tip. A subtle visual check is to note while you move into the center circle that each jumper is across from their own bench. This will ensure the jumpers are headed to the basket furthest from their team bench to begin the game.

Get Comfortable -- Whether you toss the ball with one hand or two, make sure it's a technique that you have practiced and can consistently produce a ball that rises straight and to a height the players will reach at the peak of their leap.

Stay Safe -- In the close confines of two jumpers who are leaning in and jockeying for position, it's important to stay out of the way for both your personal safety and to ensure the jumpers are not hindered in their efforts to tap the ball. Keep the whistle out of your mouth, and hold your spot so as not to step back into the action.

Keep in mind, jumpers must have both feet within the center restraining circle.

Once the Referee is ready to toss the ball, non-jumpers cannot move ONTO the circle or CHANGE POSITIONS.

Teammates may not occupy adjacent positions around the center circle **if an opponent** requests the spot before the Referee is ready to toss the ball. Until the ball is touched by one or both jumpers, the non-jumpers cannot break the plane of the circle or take a position in any occupied position.

If the toss is not touched by at least one jumper, a second toss should be administered. Also, a jumper is not required to jump, but if neither player does they both can be ordered to do so.

Neither **jumper** may:

- Touch the ball before it reaches its **highest point**.
- **Leave the circle** before the ball is touched.
- **Catch** the ball.
- Touch the ball more than **TWICE**.

Any of these results in a violation being ruled before the clock (and game) is started.

The jump ball restrictions **END** when the tapped ball contacts:

- A non-jumper.
- An official.
- The floor.
- A basket or backboard.

If you commit these jump ball tips to memory you won't have to think twice about making a good first impression in any of your officiating assignments.

Rule References
NFHS 6-3   NCAA 4.42, 6.4

Knowledge Check

The referee is ready to toss the ball to begin the game when A-1 steps back away from the center circle.

The umpire blows his whistle and rules this movement by A-1 a violation.

Is the umpire correct?

No. The movement by A-1 is legal.

Views from the Center
by Billy Martin

O fficiating as part of a three person crew, and being in the **center position** can provide some of the best views of the game in the whole arena.

The Center (official) has a complete look across the floor and playing area, while the Lead and Trail focus specifically on

the ball-side activity. The Center, in a position on the free-throw line extended just off the sideline, can watch all the players from the weak side with little or no visual obstruction.

However, that advantageous position can change in a heartbeat when the ball swings and the play comes towards the official sitting in Center position. One of the **more uncomfortable positions** occurs when the play is "right on top" of the Center and your back is up against the side-line, with nowhere to move and straight-lined behind the players.

What is a good way to **improve your position**, once this occurs?

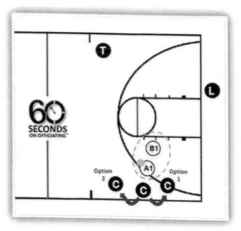

OPTION 1: Dive Down

One recommendation is taking one (or possibly two) steps down towards the endline to get a better angle on the play.

There are a couple of things to remember here.

- Make your first movement **back** toward the sideline and **then down**, as you don't want to **get <u>too close</u> to the play.** Use common sense when moving as it should improve your line of sight.

- Remember, the **lead official** has probably **closed down** by now and is contemplating (or has already) come across to initiate a rotation on this play.

If you see or "feel" the lead coming... **referee the play** and start to rotate towards the division line into the trail position which completes the crew movement.

If the **lead does not come across**, referee the play and move to improve your angle as the play develops.

OPTION 2: Draw Back

Another option is to move towards the division line on this play. Remember...

- Don't move **so far backward**, as to create a situation with two trail officials. One or two steps away from the players are usually sufficient.

- Maintain **good sight lines** and angles on this play as it could develop into a drive to the basket in your primary area.

- If the **lead does come across**, then you are already in a prime position to complete the rotation, **after** the opposite trail moves into their position as the new center.

It's always better to have a temporary situation with __two Center__ officials as opposed to officiating with __two Trails__.

Check with your conference / organization to determine the preferred method of movement in the center position. This is a great talking point for any pre-game conference when discussing primary coverage areas, live ball rotations, and cohesive movement as a crew.

Is Off the Backboard an Above Board Play?

by Tim Malloy

All officials have moments in a game where everything is going along just fine -- you're in a great rhythm and you've been positioned perfectly to see every play in your primary area -- when suddenly a player does something that catches you by surprise.

Did you blow your whistle and rule a violation on the strange play because *"it just didn't look right"*, or were you momentarily stunned and just let play continue?

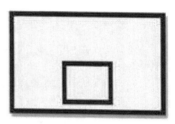

Here's an example for you to consider...

- A player with the ball is **trapped** by defenders in the lane.
- That player appears to pass the ball to himself ... by **tossing the ball** against their **own backboard**.
- That same player **recovers the ball**.

Is this a legal play?

What would be **your** ruling on this situation?

In the scenario described here you must consider several things.

- Throwing the ball and hitting the backboard of the **team in possession** is always considered a **try for goal**.

- Even though the attempt (a soft toss or a hard carom off the glass) does not look like a legitimate try for goal should have **no bearing** on your ruling.

The tossing player may compete to recover the ball, and if they do, they have the same privileges as the other nine players on the court to shoot the ball or begin a dribble.

The critical phrase here is, "**their <u>own</u> backboard**."

Same (less likely) scenario ... but at the opposite end of the court:

Throwing the ball off the <u>**opponents**</u> backboard is always considered the **start of a dribble**. When the same player catches the ball - that <u>**ends**</u> the dribble.

- If the player had **not dribbled** prior to this ... it's perfectly legal to **continue** that dribble, provided they do so before catching (or ending) that dribble.

- Also if the player had not dribbled prior, they can certainly **catch** the ball, which **ends** that dribble.

- If the player had **dribbled previously** – throwing the ball against the opponent's backboard would constitute a **2nd dribble**, thus a violation would be ruled, when **that player re-touches the ball**.

Any scenario along this line involving a player's own backboard is considered fair game to recover the ball or dribble.

And finally, just to branch out a bit further on this thought tree, keep in mind if a player makes a **legitimate attempt** for goal and the **ball does not touch** the backboard or ring:

- they may **recover the ball** to shoot again...
- or **begin a new dribble.**

If you determine the release of the ball was not a legitimate field goal attempt (to avoid being blocked or to toss it over/around the defender), recovering the ball by the same player would be a violation.

Rules Reference
NFHS Case Book 4-15-1c A & D; 4-15-4c
NCAA 4-71-4, AR 131

Knowledge Check

A dribbling A-1 is being pressured in the backcourt and attempts to pass the ball to A-2.

The pass deflects off Team B's backboard and bounces directly back to A-1. Can A-1 legally dribble?

A-1 cannot start a legal dribble after this.

Twenty Rule Concepts
You Must Know
by Billy Martin

T he following are **NFHS fundamentals** that will provide a sturdy foundation for officials to build on their knowledge of the rules governing the **scholastic** basketball games you work. Commit these principles to memory and you will no doubt perform calmly and confidently in any chaotic game situation.

NFHS RULE FUNDAMENTALS

1. While the ball remains live, a **loose ball always remains in control** of the team whose player last had control, unless it is a try or tap for goal.

2. Neither a team nor any player is **ever in control** during a dead ball, jump ball, throw-in, or when the ball is in flight during a try or tap for a goal.

3. A **goal is made** when a live ball enters the basket from above and remains in or passes through unless canceled by a throw-in violation or a player control foul.

4. The jump ball, the throw-in and the free throw are the only methods of **getting a dead ball live**.

5. Neither the **dribble nor traveling rule operates** during the jump ball, throw-on or free throw.

6. It is **not possible for a player to travel** during a dribble.

7. The only **infractions for which points are awarded** are goaltending by the defense or basket interference at the opponent's basket.

8. There are **three types of violations** and each has its own penalty.

9. A **ball in flight** has the same relationship to frontcourt or backcourt, or inbounds or out of bounds, as when it last touched a person or the floor.

10. **Personal fouls always involve illegal contact** and occur during a live ball, **except** a common foul by or on an airborne shooter.

11. The **penalty** for a single **flagrant personal** or **flagrant technical** foul is two free throws and disqualification plus awarding the ball to the opponents for a throw-in.

12. **Penalties for fouls** are **administered in the order** in which they occur.

13. A **live-ball foul by the offense** (team in control or last in control if the ball is loose), or the expiration of time for a quarter or extra period, causes the **ball to become dead immediately,** <u>unless</u> the ball is in flight during a try or tap for goal. The ball also becomes **dead when a player-control foul** occurs.

14. The **first or only free-throw violation** by the offense causes the ball to become **dead immediately**.

15. A **double personal foul** involves only personal fouls and only two opponents; **no free throws** awarded and the ball is put in play at the point of interruption. A **double technical foul** involves only technical fouls and only two opponents; **no free throws** are awarded, and the ball is put in play at the point of interruption.

16. The official's **whistle seldom causes the ball to become dead** (it is already dead).

17. "**Continuous motion**" applies both to a **try and a tap** for field goals and free throws, but it has **no significance unless** there is a foul by the defense during the interval which begins when the habitual trying or tapping movement starts and ends when the ball is clearly in flight.

18. Whether the **clock is running or is stopped** has **no influence** on the **counting of a goal**.

19. A ball which touches the **front face or edges of the backboard** is treated the same as touching the floor inbounds, **except** that when the ball touches the **thrower's backboard**, it does **not constitute** a part of a **dribble**.

20. If the ball goes through the basket before or after a **player-control foul**, the goal shall **not be counted**.

NCAA Rule Fundamentals
by Al Battista

If you are an official who works a blended schedule of high school and **NCAA men's contests**, please keep in mind these important differences when working at the collegiate level:

NCAA RULE FUNDAMENTALS
(Compared to NFHS)

- There is a 35-second **shot clock**.
- Players lined up for a free throw attempt(s) may enter the foul lane area **on the release** of the ball by the free throw shooter.
- Overtime periods are **five-minutes** in duration.
- The **game clock will stop** after a made basket in the last 59.9 seconds of the second-half, or any overtime period.
- An **airborne player cannot call timeout** to avoid a backcourt or out-of-bounds violation.
- **Timeouts** for non-media games: Four x 75 Second and Two x 30 Second timeouts available.
- The team calling timeout can shorten the length of the stoppage and resume play (sound horn, plus 15 seconds).

- Once the ball **touches the backboard above the ring**, the ball is considered on its downward flight. Any contact to the ball is to be ruled goaltending.
- If a team trainer determines blood on a player's jersey is **"non-saturated"** the player may continue to wear the jersey without interruption.
- A player who swings his elbows and makes contact with an opponent **above the shoulders** is to be charged with, at a minimum, an **intentional foul**. Below the shoulder contact from a player swinging his elbows, can/may be charged with a player control foul.
- Technical fouls are designated as Class "A" and Class "B" and play is resumed at the **point of interruption**.
- Class "B" technical fouls (grasping the ring, dunking a dead ball, delay of game, slapping the backboard) **do not count** towards a player's disqualification or the team's bonus.
- The **opposing coach** will select a player on the floor to shoot the awarded free throws of an injured player who is unable to continue the result of a common foul. The coach of the injured player may select anyone on his team to shoot the awarded free throws caused by an intentional or flagrant foul.

Please commit these critical differences to memory and your movement to and from the high school and college ranks will be with considerably less stress.

Inbounding During a Transition
by Billy Martin

I n a **two person crew** during a quick transition from the backcourt to the frontcourt -- sometimes the ball will be deflected out of bounds by the defense on the **lead official's sideline** (while transitioning).

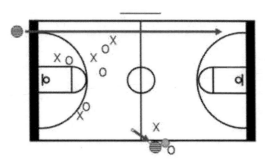

Example 1: Ball is deflected out in the frontcourt closest to the transitioning lead.

Depending on **where** the ball kicks out ... determines **who** will administer the throw-in.

Here's a couple easy ways to remember and review during your two person crew pre-game. In these scenarios **YOU are the LEAD**.

"Whenever the ball goes out of bounds in the **front court** - if **you blow** the line ... then **you inbound** the ball."

In figure 1, the ball kicks out in the front court as the new lead is transitioning down the court. Blow the line and handle the ball which causes the old trail to become the new lead. It's a long run but is consistent with other front court mechanics in a two person crew.

"Whenever the ball goes out of bounds in the **backcourt** – regardless of who blows (the line) -- the **trail will always inbound** the ball."

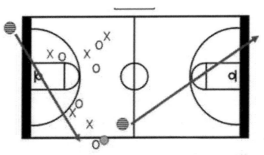

Example 2: Ball goes out of bounds in the backcourt during transition.

In Example 2, the new lead is up helping (versus the press) on the sideline while Team A is in transition. The ball is deflected out of bounds (by Team B) and the ball is awarded back to Team A, still heading up court in the same direction.

Here, proper mechanics would be to give up the inbounds to the **trail** who administers **all lines in the backcourt.**

The same mechanics apply to the crew in a standard front court set. If you blow a line in the front court you will administer the throw in.

Talk about this in your two person crew pre-game and your dead ball efficiency will be maximized.

Reference: LAABO Mechanics Manual

Crossing the Line
by Tim Malloy

Whenever you hear about someone *"crossing the line,"* it's a safe bet that person is likely in a bit of trouble on the job or in a relationship.

Well the same can be said about a player who crosses the line in a **scholastic (NFHS)** basketball game. More specifically, when a player reaches through the **boundary-line**  plane on a sideline or end line and disrupts the opponent during a throw-in.

Let's look at the implications to the defender for **crossing the boundary-line plane:**

- If a **defender reaches through** the boundary-line plane, but makes **no contact**, the official will issue a **delay of game warning** to the **defensive team.**

- Any **additional violations** for reaching through the boundary-line plane, **without contact,** will result in a **technical foul** being charged against the defending **team** (**not** the player.)

If a **defender reaches through** the boundary-line plane, and **makes contact with the ball**, the official will issue a **technical foul** against the **defender.** No warning is required.

This includes reaching through the plane of the end line and **intercepting a pass** to another offensive player who has stepped out-of-bounds while attempting to complete the throw-in.

If a **defender reaches through** the boundary-line plane, and **makes contact with the thrower**, the official will issue an **intentional personal foul** against the defender.

However, if the **player attempting the throw-in breaks the boundary-line plane** with the ball:

- The **defender may legally slap or grab the ball** out of the offensive player's hands.
- If **both players have a firm grasp** on the ball, a **held ball is called** resulting in an **alternating possession** throw-in.

If the original throw-in was an alternating possession throw-in, the offensive team **maintains the arrow** following the held ball.

So while we can't offer any advice if you find you have crossed the line in your personal or professional life, we hope we have clarified what to do if player crosses the line in a game you are officiating!

Rule Reference
NFHS: 10.1.10 and 10.3.10

Clearly Out of Bounds
by Tim Malloy and Billy Martin

As officials we all realize that a player shall not cause the ball to go out of bounds or be out of bounds when he/she touches the ball or this will be ruled a violation.

Here are a couple of uncommon **Out of Bounds** plays that we should keep our eyes open for in order to rule properly on when they occur.

The obvious stuff outside the boundary lines...

- Ball touches / touched by any person (including non-players) = Out of Bounds
- Ball strikes an object (i.e. ceiling,light fixtures,side baskets) = Out of Bounds
- Ball touches an official standing on (or outside boundary line)= Out of Bounds
- The player last to touch the ball would have caused the violation.

How about the rectangular backboard ...

- If the ball passes OVER the backboard = Violation.
- Ball touches any support structure or guide wires = Violation
- Ball touches the back of the backboard = Violation
- Ball touches the top, the bottom, or side edges of backboard = OK

Player jumping back onto the court ...

- Location of an airborne player is the same as when the player was in last contact with the floor.
- The key to remember here is ... "you only need one foot inbounds before he/she TOUCHES the ball to be legal."
- Look for the foot and determine which happened first ... foot touching floor or hands touching ball. Foot touches first (inbounds), then it's a good play.

Player jumping to save the ball from going out of bounds...

- Watch the feet of the player jumping **prior** to touching the ball.
- Did the player jump from completely inbounds?
- Or, did they leap from out of bounds (or foot touching the boundary line)?
- Blow the whistle immediately when the player touches the ball to save it if they were not completely inbounds prior to the jumping.

Dribbler stepping on the boundary line (or out of bounds)...

The key here is a player that steps on the boundary line while dribbling is considered out of bounds even if their hand is not in contact with the ball.

When in doubt, use the AP Arrow ...

Play shall be resumed by the team entitled to the next Alternating Possession throw-in at the closest spot to the violation if:

- the touching by two opponents (simultaneously) causes the ball to go out of bounds ...
- Or, if the official is in doubt as to who last touched the ball ...
- Or, if two officials disagree who caused the violation ...

Note ... if the simultaneous violation occurs on a jump ball (to start the game / overtime period) BEFORE the AP Procedure is established, make sure to resume play with another jump ball between the two opponents that caused the violation (NFHS ONLY). It might not be the original two jumpers!

In closing, when a player leaves the court for an unauthorized reason -like avoiding a screen to gain an advantage -- this is not an "out of bounds" violation.

Just blow your whistle to cause the ball to become dead and point to the spot of the violation while communicating this is a "leaving the court" violation.

Though it may be subtle, these are two different violations which carry the same penalty ... the other team is awarded the ball at the nearest spot.

NFHS Reference
9-3-1 and 2, 7-1-1 and 2,4-35-1 and 2, 9-3-3

Make sure you take a moment and subscribe to our **FREE** newsletter for timely updates to the basketball community through these online outlets:

60 Seconds on Officiating Website
(free in-season email newsletter)
www.ref60.com
www.refereelife.com

Beyond the Rules Book Website
www.gobeyondtherules.com

Facebook
Search for: 60 Seconds on Officiating

Twitter
@Ref60

LinkedIn
Search for: 60 Seconds on Officiating

We at *60 Seconds on Officiating* wish you an abundance of great health and great games this season and beyond!

Al Battista
Tim Malloy
Billy Martin

Thank-you for the continued support from our educational partners.

INTERNATIONAL ASSOCIATION
OF APPROVED BASKETBALL OFFICIALS
www.iaabo.org

Through a worldwide organization of some 200 local "Boards" spanning 38 States and 11 foreign counties, IAABO has been the unparalleled and undisputed leader in worldwide training of basketball officials for over 85 years.

Made in the USA
San Bernardino, CA
08 May 2018